PRAISE FOR

TWO OR THREE THINGS
I KNOW FOR SURE

"Captures Allison's raw gifts as a storyteller. . . . She ponders the uses and limits of fiction in a world where truth can be the most brutal story of all."

—*The New York Times Book Review*

"A model memoir, harrowing in its depiction of family truths, however painful . . . generous to others and unsparing of the author, and written in simple language that verges toward a kind of rough-hewn poetry."

—*Seattle Post-Intelligencer*

"Any time she says, 'Let me tell you a story,' all she has to do is name the time and the place. I'll be there."

—Geoffrey Stokes, *The Boston Sunday Globe*

"Her stories—and life—are a triumph of love over cruelty. Read it aloud and savor the rhythms."

—*Publishers Weekly*

"A book of wisdom, a book of medicines. . . . One feels the vicious, devouring cycle of rage and pain defeated."

—*Los Angeles Times Book Review*

DOROTHY ALLISON is the National Book Award finalist and bestselling author of the novel *Bastard Out of Carolina; Cavedweller; Trash; Skin: Talking About Sex, Class and Literature;* and *The Women Who Hate Me.* She lives in northern California.

Also by the author:

Skin: Talking About Sex, Class and Literature

Bastard Out of Carolina

Cavedweller

Trash

The Women Who Hate Me

Dorothy Allison

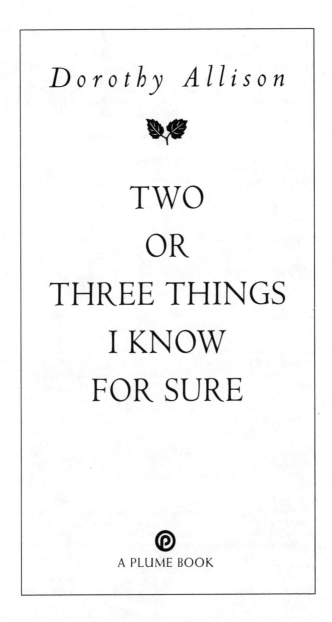

TWO
OR
THREE THINGS
I KNOW
FOR SURE

A PLUME BOOK

PLUME
Published by the Penguin Group
Penguin Books USA Inc., 375 Hudson Street, New York, New York 10014, U.S.A.
Penguin Books Ltd, 27 Wrights Lane, London W8 5TZ, England
Penguin Books Australia Ltd, Ringwood, Victoria, Australia
Penguin Books Canada Ltd, 10 Alcorn Avenue, Toronto, Ontario, Canada M4V 3B2
Penguin Books (N.Z.) Ltd, 182–190 Wairau Road, Auckland 10, New Zealand

Penguin Books Ltd, Registered Offices: Harmondsworth, Middlesex, England

Published by Plume, an imprint of Dutton Signet,
a division of Penguin Books USA Inc.
Previously published in a Dutton edition.

First Plume Printing, August, 1996
30 29 28 27

Ⓟ REGISTERED TRADEMARK—MARCA REGISTRADA

The Library of Congress has catalogued the Dutton edition as follows:

Allison, Dorothy.
    Two or three things I know for sure / Dorothy Allison.
        p.   cm.
    ISBN 0-525-93921-0 (hc.)
    ISBN 0-452-27340-4 (pbk.)
    1. Allison, Dorothy—Drama.   2. Women authors, American—20th century—
Drama.   3. Poor women—United States—Drama.   4. Feminists—United
States—Drama.   5. Lesbians—United States—Drama.   6. Family—
United States—Drama.   I. Title.
PS3551.L453Z476   1995
812'.54—dc20   95–17752
                                                                      CIP

Printed in the United States of America
Original hardcover design by Steven N. Stathakis

For my sisters

TWO
OR
THREE THINGS
I KNOW
FOR SURE

"LET ME TELL YOU A STORY," I used to whisper to my sisters, hiding with them behind the red-dirt bean hills and row on row of strawberries. My sisters' faces were thin and sharp, with high cheekbones and restless eyes, like my mama's face, my aunt Dot's, my own. Peasants, that's what we are and always have been. Call us the lower orders, the great unwashed, the working class, the poor, proletariat, trash, lowlife and scum. I can make a story out of it, out of us. Make it pretty or sad, laughable or haunting. Dress it up with legend and aura and romance.

"Let me tell you a story," I'd begin, and start another one. When we were small, I could catch my sisters the way they caught butterflies, capture their attention and almost make them believe that all I said was true. "Let me tell you about the women who ran away. All those legendary women who ran away." I'd tell about the witch queens who cooked their enemies in great open pots, the jewels that grow behind the tongues of water moccasins. After a while the deepest satisfaction was in the story itself, greater even than the terror in my sisters' faces, the laughter, and, God help us, the hope.

The constant query of my childhood was "Where you been?" The answer, "Nowhere." Neither my stepfather nor my mother believed me. But no punishment could discover another answer. The truth was that I did go nowhere—nowhere in particular and everywhere imaginable. I walked and told myself stories, walked out of our subdivision and into another, walked all the way to the shopping center and then back. The flush my mama suspected hid an afternoon of shoplifting or vandalism was simple embarrassment, because when I walked, I talked—story-talked, out loud—assuming identities I made up. Sometimes I was myself, arguing loudly as I could never do at home. Sometimes I became people I had seen on television or read about in books, went places I'd barely heard of, did things that no one I knew had ever done, particularly things that girls were not supposed to do. In the world as I remade it, nothing was forbidden; everything was possible.

I'll tell you a story and maybe you'll believe me.

There's a laboratory in the basement of the Greenville County General Hospital, I told my sisters. They take the babies down there. If you're poor—from the wrong family, the wrong color, the wrong side of town—they mess with you, alter your brain. That was what happened. That was it.

You believe me?

I'm a storyteller. I'll work to make you believe me. Throw in some real stuff, change a few details, add the certainty of outrage. I know the use of fiction in a world of hard truth, the way fiction can be a harder piece of truth. The story of what happened, or what did not happen but should have—that story can become a curtain drawn shut, a piece of insulation, a disguise, a razor, a tool that changes every time it is used and sometimes becomes something other than we intended.

The story becomes the thing needed.

Two or three things I know for sure, and one of them is what it means to have no loved version of your life but the one you make.

LET ME TELL YOU A STORY. If I could convince myself, I can convince you. But you were not there when I began. You were not the one I was convincing. When I began there were just nightmares and need and stubborn determination.

When I began there was only the suspicion that making up the story as you went along was the way to survive. And if I know anything, I know how to survive, how to remake the world in story.

But where am I in the stories I tell? Not the storyteller but the woman in the story, the woman who believes in story. What is the truth about her? She was one of them, one of those legendary women who ran away. A witch queen, a warrior maiden, a mother with a canvas suitcase, a daughter with broken bones. Women run away because they must. I ran because if I had not, I would have died. No one told me that you take your world with you, that running becomes a habit, that the secret to running is to know why you run and where you are going—and to leave behind the reason you run.

My mama did not run away. My aunt Dot and aunt Grace and cousin Billie with her near dozen children—they did not run. They learned resilience and determination and the cost of hard compromises. None of them ever intended to lose their lives or their children's lives, to be trapped by those hard compromises and ground down until they no longer knew who they were, what they had first intended. But it happened. It happened over and over again.

Aunt Dot was the one who said it. She said, "Lord, girl, there's only two or three things I know for sure." She put her head back, grinned, and made a small impatient noise. Her eyes glittered as bright as sun reflecting off the scales of a cottonmouth's back. She spat once and shrugged. "Only two or three things. That's right," she said. "Of course it's never the same things, and I'm never as sure as I'd like to be."

Where I was born—Greenville, South Carolina—
smelled like nowhere else I've ever been. Cut wet
grass, split green apples, baby shit and beer bottles,
cheap makeup and motor oil. Everything was ripe,
everything was rotting. Hound dogs butted my
calves. People shouted in the distance; crickets
boomed in my ears. That country was beautiful, I
swear to you, the most beautiful place I've ever
been. Beautiful and terrible. It is the country of

my dreams and the country of my nightmares: a pure pink and blue sky, red dirt, white clay, and all that endless green—willows and dogwood and firs going on for miles.

Two or three things I know for sure, and one of them is the way you can both hate and love something you are not sure you understand.

🌿 IN GREENVILLE, halfway through the fourth grade, we got a substitute teacher right out of college and full of ideas. First she brought in a record player and got us to sing along to folk songs—"Cum by yah, my lord, cum by yah!"—until another teacher complained of the noise. Next she tried to get us to do news reports, each of us presenting something we had learned from the news the night before. Another time, it might have worked, but the nightly news was full of Birmingham and Little Rock, burning buses and freedom marchers. Our reports degenerated into shouting matches and mortal insults, voices raised in more than song. More complaints, and this time the principal came around.

Our teacher fell back on what seemed an utterly safe choice. We were to make our family trees, interviewing relatives and doing posters to show the class.

"You can check family Bibles for the names of previous generations, and if you've got pictures, you could glue them on the posters." She blew hard on a strand of hair that had fallen over her right eye. Teaching was clearly not what she had expected. "Or you can make drawings or even cut pictures out of magazines to represent people— anything you like. This is where you get to be creative. Make something your families are going to want to keep."

We watched as she rummaged through her skirt pockets until she found a hairpin. She spoke while using both hands to tuck her hair back into a rough bun. "Any questions?"

"She wants you to what?" Mama's tone was pure exasperation when I came home that afternoon. She'd been talking with Aunt Dot, spreading clothes on the dining room table, getting them all sprinkled and rolled up before settling down to ironing. Now she looked like she was ready to throw something.

"This girl an't from around here. Is she?" From the other side of the table Aunt Dot gave Mama a quick grin over the rim of her coffee cup. "I can just see all those children putting down Mama's name, and first daddy's name and second daddy's name. Could get complicated."

"Dot!"

"Well, you know I'm right. That brand-new teacher an't gonna last out the month. Around here parentage is even more dangerous than politics."

"Why is it so dangerous?"

"Girl, you getting too big to ask silly questions."

"Well, I need to make lists. I need people's names. Where's our family Bible?"

"Our what? Lord. Lord." Aunt Dot waved one hand in the air. "Girl is definitely not from around here."

"We don't have a family Bible?"

"Child, some days we don't even have a family."

"Dot, don't get started." Mama folded the sleeves of a damp shirt in over the button front, and then, gathering from the collar, rolled the whole into a closed tube. "And you just put down what you know."

"What do I know? Aunt Grace said once that Granny had eleven children. I know six."

"Eleven?" Aunt Dot took a sip from her cup and propped her chin on her palm. "Was it eleven? I thought it was nine."

"Well, nine! I still only know six."

"There's no need to count the dead." Mama snapped a work shirt open and sprinkled furiously. "Put down who you know. You don't have to put down everybody."

"But you're supposed to."

"Dorothy." Her expression stopped me. I knew that look. One more word and I would be in trouble.

"Well, I don't have Grandpa Gibson's name."

Dot put her cup down noisily. "Andrew, right?"

"Andrew James."

"So, Andrew James Gibson and Mattie Lee."

"Andrew James Gibson and Mattie Lee Garner. Now, that's enough."

I gathered up my papers and headed out the door. From the carport, I heard Aunt Dot's booming laugh. "What you think? Should we get a family Bible?"

Two or three things I know for sure, and one of them is just this—if we cannot name our own we are cut off at the root, our hold on our lives as fragile as seed in a wind.

MY MAMA DIED AT MIDNIGHT ON A SATURDAY. My sister Anne was with her, holding her hands and trying to tell her we were on our way. My sister Wanda and I were miles away, lost in the parking garage at the Orlando airport. I had just flown in from Buffalo, shaking still with the effort of trying to make the plane go faster by sheer will.

"We have to hurry," Wanda told me, and gave that bark of a laugh that meant nothing was funny. We ran. We dodged tourists and baggage handlers, squalling children and panhandlers for Jesus. "Get out of the way!" I yelled at a guy in a pale blue suit.

"No need to be rude, sister," he said in a voice that any other day would have cut me to the quick.

In the parking garage we got lost. Wanda glared across the rows of economy vehicles, cursing, saying, "Damn, this doesn't look right. Damn city growing so fast. Goddammit, this doesn't look right."

The elevator wasn't working at all, and Wanda was only half sure we were in the right building. She kept shoving doors open, throwing herself into another staircase, and dragging me up another level, up three before she finally recognized the half-finished color coding.

"There!" she yelled. "Right there." And I saw her Ford, recognizable at a glance by the tinted windows and the fuzz-buster duct-taped to the dash, parked sideways in its slot. I laughed then—at the car, at Wanda, at the comedy of it all, Wanda hiding her fear behind outrage while I could do nothing but shake my head and follow close behind.

After, I kept thinking that it must have been that moment when Mama reached to grab Anne's hand for the last time, when her mouth—no longer speaking what her mind was seeing—began that soft wordless howl. Twenty minutes of howling and then silence, and death happening then like the closing of a book.

"You mean and stubborn and completely Ruth's daughter," Aunt Dot had told me when I visited her years ago and would not give her the gossip about Mama that she wanted. I had made a

mantra of her words. "Mean and stubborn and Ruth's daughter. I don't hold grudges. I kick butt and keep moving. Mean and stubborn and Ruth Gibson's daughter." But what did that mean in a world without her? Who were Ruth Gibson's daughters without her?

After the good-byes and the weeping, walking away from the hospital together, my sisters and I became other people. All through the funeral rituals, we acted as if we had become careful strangers. I imagined myself crisp and efficient, doing what seemed necessary, barely pausing to wipe the tears I could not stop. Anne walked silently through the motions, white-faced and wounded, though the air around her hummed and burned. It was Wanda, my big sister, who startled me, putting me down in her own bed, serving food I didn't know she knew how to cook, teasing the relatives out of their animosity. She even got my uncle Brice to talk to my aunt Maudy and kept me carefully out of my stepfather's reach.

At first I wasn't sure what my sister was doing, but at the funeral home I began to understand. We had gone through Mama's things together, talked about buying something special, but finally chosen clothes for Mama that she had worn and loved—her lucky shirt, loose-fitting cotton trousers, and her most comfortable shoes. "Only woman ever buried in her bingo outfit," I would tell friends later. But choosing those clothes, we had not laughed; we had felt guided by what Mama would have wanted. It was when I watched Wanda fasten Mama's lucky necklace—the little silver racehorse positioned in the hollow of Mama's throat—that I saw.

Wanda was being Mama, doing what Mama

would have done, comforting us the way only Mama had known to do. I looked around and saw Anne holding my stepfather's shoulder as he sobbed, looked down and saw my own hands locked on the little bag of Mama's jewelry we had found in her dresser. For a moment I wanted to cry, and then I didn't. Of all the things I had imagined, this was the one I had not foreseen. We had become Mama.

I reached past my sister to put my hand on Mama's face, to touch her again and push away my sudden fear. But the cheek was hard and cold, something marble and inhuman. I did not know then what was more terrifying—what my mama had become or what we had.

We divided Mama's things among us.

My sisters have daughters. I insisted they take all the jewelry to pass on, but it was no great gesture. My mama had nothing worth any money, only one good bracelet and one good ring that I pressed on Anne and Wanda. They insisted I take the engagement band. It was cold in my hand. I tucked it in a little satin bag in which Mama had kept three spools of thread, tiny plated scissors, needles, and a thimble. A month later,

in Los Angeles to do a reading, I would lose the bag, the ring, all my clothes, and the manuscript I was completing. But when I told my sisters about it, all I thought was that the sewing bag was the only thing Mama had owned that I really wanted.

Then I remembered the pictures.

For two decades, every time I visited, I shuffled through those pictures—scores of ancient snapshots stuffed in a box in the end table in Mama's living room. Each time I pulled them out and asked Mama to go through them with me. The faces in Mama's box were full of stories—ongoing tragedies, great novels, secrets and mysteries and longings no one would ever know.

"Who's this?" I would ask about another cracked and fading sepia image of a child.

"That was your cousin that drowned."

"And this?"

"She was the one ran off at thirteen. Now, what was her name?"

It was the ones no one remembered who pulled at me. Two women with bright-faced toddlers on their laps bracketed a sullen adolescent girl. Her hair pinned up on the crown of her head. Theirs was long and loose. All had the same eyes, the same eyebrows.

"Didn't she marry Bo?" Mama's finger traced the smile of the woman on the left. "This is her girl beside her, and the babies they both had the same year." Mama flattened her lips and touched the face of the girl on the side where it was obscured by a flaw in the print.

"Don't think I ever knew the other daughter." Her lips parted as if she were about to say something, but she stopped and gave a slight shake of her head.

"Were they the ones who died in the bridge accident?" I reached for the photograph, but Mama pulled it away.

"What accident?"

"The one Granny told me about."

"Oh, you know your granny."

"Then what did happen?"

Mama's grip on the photograph tightened, the tips of her fingers going white while her mouth set in a thin hard line. "Nothing happened to them," she said. "Nothing at all."

Mama would touch the pictures tentatively, as if her memories were more real than the images, as if she did not want to look too hard at the reality of all those people lost and gone. Every time I asked, she promised that as soon as she found a spare moment, she would go through the box, sort through the photos, and write it all down, each name, each fate she could remember. Every time, seeing the way her hands moved on those snapshots, I knew it wasn't likely that she would keep her promise.

Now spread across Wanda's coffee table, they were as anonymous as they had been all my life. My aunt Bodine went through them, but she seemed to know as little as I. "Never met her; don't think I knew him."

There were a few she did know. "Oh, that's your aunt Dot, your granny, and the boys, David

and Dan. Your cousins Billie and Bobbie. Your uncle Brice, the handsome one, and this one's him with his best friend died in the Korean War. Your mama at fifteen, I think, and this one at sixteen."

My mother was beautiful, that hard thing, beautiful. Men wanted my mama, wanted her before she knew what it meant, when she was twelve, thirteen, still a child. She showed me once that snapshot of herself at fifteen; white socks and A-line skirt, hair in a Kitty Wells cloud, schoolgirl blouse, Peter Pan collar, and the most hesitant smile.

"Just a girl," Mama said, shrugging. "I was just a girl."

"Pregnant," my aunt Dot told me, "carrying you then. That was taken just before she ran off with that silly boy."

That beautiful boy my mama loved, as skinny as her, as ignorant and hungry, as proud as he could be to have that beautiful girl, her skin full of heat, her eyes full of hope. And when he ran away, left her to raise me alone, she never trusted any man again—but wanted to, wanted to so badly it ate the heart out of her.

"WE COULD BE RELATED," Lucy told me. She'd been living in Monte Rio a little longer than I had, and we'd see each other mornings when I walked down to the post office. I would sit with her on the bench under the post office window and watch the way she used her hands. She kept pushing her hair back, dark brown hair in a thick dry mass covering her neck and shoulders.

"I'm a Campbell on my granddaddy's side," Lucy told me proudly. "And a Gibson, I'm pretty sure, from a great-aunt I never actually met. My real name is Lillian, though people around here don't know that. I don't think anybody in the world knows anymore." She stopped and stared off into the distance, as if she were looking for someone who remembered her from when she was Lillian.

"My people moved to Arkansas," Lucy said. "I changed my name when I married P. J. He didn't like Lillian." And then she told the rest of it, how she left Arkansas at twenty-two, running away from P.J. and a load of debt. As she spoke, Lucy's face changed, seemed to become painfully flat and hard, as if the morning sun had shifted in the sky, throwing no shadows to soften the line of brow or chin.

"Got on the Greyhound with two suitcases and a little patent leather handbag. Had me two Cokes and a fifth of Ancient Age bourbon, what P.J. called the poor man's Jack Daniel's. Nursed that whiskey across the whole Southwest, all the way to Arizona. But I came into Bakersfield sober, cold sober and crying. Lord damn, I think I cried straight through the first few weeks. Didn't look back, couldn't never look back. It was either kill the man or leave, and it wasn't worth killing him."

She stopped and looked around as if the change in the light had finally registered on her, too. "I'm cold," she said. "You cold?"

She left him the furniture, the truck, and the house on a quarter acre of scrub oak. On the worked-pine dining room table his parents had given them, she left him the reason she was leaving—the hospital bill for their stillborn daughter, the one he had insisted didn't matter. *"It wasn't like it was a boy."*

"Son of a bitch," she said.

"I got a problem, you know, same old same old." She laughed a familiar bitter laugh and looked at me sideways. "But I been clean a week now, and I'm doing good. It an't easy like people pretend, changing your life this late in. An't easy at all."

She laughed again, smoothing the fabric of her loose trousers. "Hell, though, nothing is, is it?" And I laughed with her, not reminding her of last month or the month before. Every time I run into her we have the same conversation, how she's getting clean—working at it, anyway—and doing good, doing good until she isn't. Then she gets drunk again and sings to the trees.

When Lucy drinks she plays records and swears if she'd just had the chance she too could have been a country star. Maybe so. Sometimes when I hear her voice in the distance, I believe her, that contralto drifting up into the redwood trees as pure and clean as her rage ever was.

Maybe we *are* related. Among my mama's photos there was one woman with a face similar to Lucy's, another handsome woman with a dark cloud of hair, one of my mama's aunts, I think. But Lucy's drawl is Barstow, not Greenville. She spent five years in Bakersfield. Now she roasts turkey stuffed with jalapeño peppers, deep-fries artichoke hearts, and loves to make a salad of sliced pineapple and avocado.

"Where'd you learn to cook like this?" I asked her one afternoon.

"Family talent," she tells me. "Just picked it up as I went along." And she tries to get me to put a little whiskey in my fruit juice or at least have a beer to keep her company. The stories she tells then take me back three decades and would scare me sober if I let her make me drink.

My mama never told me stories. She might repeat something someone had said at work that day, or something she had said—lessons in how to talk back, stand up for myself, and tell someone off. But behind her blunt account of the day's conversation was a mystery: the rest of her life.

Mostly my aunts respected Mama's sense of

propriety. They wouldn't tell stories she didn't want them to tell, nothing of my father or the husband she had loved and lost. Only my grandmother was shameless.

Mattie Lee Gibson would tell people anything. Sometimes she even told the truth. She was the one told me I had an uncle who killed his wife, but said she didn't know if she believed his story about it, how he'd walked in on the woman in bed with another man. She was the one told me my mama had been married three times. My mama worked forty years as a waitress, teasing quarters out of truckers, and dimes out of

CITY HEALTH DEPARTMENT
ORLANDO, FLORIDA

N⁰ 19971

DATE

4-25-63

(OVER)

hairdressers, pouring extra coffee for a nickel, or telling an almost true story for half a dollar.

"Get them talking," she told me when she took me to work with her. "Or just smiling. Get them to remember who you are. People who recognize you will think twice before walking away and leaving nothing by the plate."

Mama was never confused about who she was or what she was offering across that counter. "It's just a job. People need their lunch served with a smile and a quick hand. Don't need to know your business—if you're tired or sick or didn't get any sleep for worrying. Just smile and get them what they need."

Three bouts of cancer and half a dozen other serious illnesses—not to mention three daughters and four grandchildren who courted trouble with every turn of the moon—but few of Mama's customers knew how stubbornly she had to put on that smile for them. She was an actress in the theater of true life, so good that no one suspected what was hidden behind the artfully applied makeup and carefully pinned hairnet.

"You should have been in the movies, like Barbara Stanwyck or Susan Hayward," I told her once as we looked at those pictures of her as a girl.

She just shook her head. "Life an't the movies," she told me.

Mama always said I was tenderhearted, I trusted too easily and would have to learn things the hard way. She was right, of course, and the thing I learned was the thing she knew intuitively: the use of charm, the art of acting, the way to turn misery into something people find understandable or sympathetic. Theater was what Mama knew and I learned.

Theater is standing up terrified and convincing people you know what you're doing—eating oysters with a smile when the only fish you've known has been canned tuna or catfish fried in cornmeal. Theater is going to bars with strangers whose incomes are four times your own; it's wearing denim when everyone around you is in silk, or silk when they're all wearing leather. Theater is talking about sex with enormous enthusiasm when nobody's ever let you in their pants. Theater is pretending you know what you're doing when you don't know anything for certain and what you do know seems to be changing all the time.

Six days out of seven I am a creation, someone who relies on luck, lust, and determination. The problem is that I know sometimes luck doesn't hold. That's when I become my mama—a woman who could charm time out of bill collectors, sympathy out of sheriffs, and love out of a man who had no heart to share.

The tragedy of the men in my family was silence, a silence veiled by boasting and jokes. If you didn't look close you might miss the sharp glint of pain in their eyes, the restless angry way they gave themselves up to fate.

My uncles went to jail like other boys go to high school. They took up girls like other people choose a craft. In my mama's photos they stare out directly, uncompromising, arms crossed or braced on their knees. I thought them beautiful and frightening, as dangerous for those quick endearing grins as for those fast muscled arms, too tall, too angry, and grown up way too soon. I remember my cousins as boys who seemed in a matter of weeks to become hard-faced men. Their eyes pulled in and closed over. Their smiles became sharp, their hands always open and ready to fight. They boasted of girls they'd had and men they'd get, ass they'd kick and trouble they'd make, talked so big and mean it was impossible to know what they meant and what they didn't. They wanted legend and adventure, wanted the stories told about the uncles to be put aside for stories about them.

"Just boys," Mattie Lee said of them. And so they remained all their lives.

Mama always loved the pictures of her mama and the twins, grandsons who towered over Mattie Lee. In one snapshot they were braced elbow to elbow, each cradling a newborn baby girl, and in their outside arms, held as tenderly as the infants, rifles extending up into the sky.

Sitting in a honky-tonk, in a clean white shirt and polished boots, hair slicked back and

teeth shining white in a dark tanned face, my uncle is the same man who leans on his knee in another photo, bare arms streaked with dirt, and a cloth cap covering his sweat-grimed brow.

"An't he a sexy man?" my cousin Billie teased. "Kind of evil-minded and quick to please. All them girlfriends half his age, and that reputation of his, like no woman ever turned him down. Wouldn't think he'd wind up living in a one-room trailer in his sister's backyard. Where'd they go, all them girlfriends and good times? What happened, you think, to that man everyone wanted to bed or marry?"

I fingered the photo and remembered one night when I was a tiny girl sleeping on the couch with my head pillowed on Mama's thigh. I had woken up to her whispering and shifting on that creaky old sofa, the taint of whiskey and tobacco smoke telling me that someone was there, and the hoarse sobs that followed confusing me, for I had never before heard my uncle cry.

"What am I gonna do?" he had said then. "Ruth, I can't stand this. I don't want to live without her. I don't think I can."

She had pulled his head into her neck, hugging him close and whispering. "You'll be all right," she said.

"Yes," he said. "I know, yes. But in the middle of the night, it feels like my heart is coming out of my chest."

She kissed his forehead, said only, "I worry about you." He shook his head hard, making her flinch from his sudden movement.

"You afraid of me?" he demanded, and she shook her head. But for a moment something burned in the cool night air.

"I just worry," she said again.

"Don't worry about me." He ran his hands down his face as if he were not actually wiping away tears, then pushed himself up off the table. "Hell, I'm a man. I can handle it."

His voice was gravel rough. He was still a handsome man but at that moment he reminded me of a painting in the Sunday school lesson book, a picture of the murdered John the Baptist, his face drained of color and pulled thin with despair. For the rest of my life I would not see him without remembering the way he looked on that night—a man who had lost the woman he loved, and with her his belief in his own life.

Two or three things I know for sure, and one of them is that no one is as hard as my uncles had to pretend to be.

LET ME TELL YOU about what I have never been allowed to be. Beautiful and female. Sexed and sexual. I was born trash in a land where the people all believe themselves natural aristocrats. Ask any white Southerner. They'll take you back two generations, say, "Yeah, we had a plantation." The hell we did.

I have no memories that can be bent so easily. I know where I come from, and it is not that part of the world. My family has a history of death and murder, grief and denial, rage and ugliness—the women of my family most of all.

The women of my family were measured, manlike, sexless, bearers of babies, burdens, and

contempt. My family? The women of my family? We are the ones in all those photos taken at mining disasters, floods, fires. We are the ones in the background with our mouths open, in print dresses or drawstring pants and collarless smocks, ugly and old and exhausted. Solid, stolid, wide-hipped baby machines. We were all wide-hipped and predestined. Wide-faced meant stupid. Wide hands marked workhorses with dull hair and tired eyes, thumbing through magazines full of women so different from us they could have been another species.

I remember standing on the porch with my aunt Maudy brushing out my hair; I was feeling loved and safe and happy. My aunt turned me around and smoothed my hair down, looked me in

the eye, smiled, and shook her head. "Lucky you're smart," she said.

Brown-toothed, then toothless, my aunt Dot showed me what I could expect.

"You're like me," she announced when she saw my third-grade school picture. "Got that nothing-gonna-stop-you look about you, girl."

I studied the picture. All I saw was another grinning girl in dark-framed glasses, missing a tooth.

"No, look." She produced a picture I would find later among Mama's treasures. In this one Aunt Dot was a smooth-skinned teenager with a wide jaw and a straightforward glare, sturdy and fearless at fifteen as she would be three decades later.

"I see," I assured her, keeping my head down and away from her demanding eyes.

What I saw was a woman who had never been beautiful and never allowed herself to care. When she found me once, red-faced and tearful, brooding over rude boys who shouted insults and ran away, she told me to wipe my face and pay no attention.

"It never changes," she said in her gravelly voice. "Men and boys, they all the same. Talk about us like we dogs, bitches sprung full-grown on the world, like we were never girls, never little babies in

[35]

our daddy's arms. Turn us into jokes 'cause we get worn down and ugly. Never look at themselves. Never think about what they're doing to girls they've loved, girls they wore out. Their girls."

"You ugly old woman," my grandfather called my grandmother.

"You ugly old woman," all my uncles called all my aunts.

"You ugly bitch," my cousins called their sisters, and my sisters called me.

"You ugly thing!" I screamed back.

The pretty girls in my high school had good hair, curled or straightened to fit the fashion, had slender hips in tailored skirts, wore virgin pins on the right side or knew enough not to wear such tacky things at all. My cousins and I were never virgins, even when we were. Like the stories told about Janis Joplin in Port Arthur, Texas, there were stories about us in Greenville, South Carolina. The football players behind the bleachers, boys who went on to marry and do well.

"Hell, it wasn't rape. She never said no. Maybe she said stop, but in that little bitty voice, so you know she wants you to love her, hell, love her for ten minutes or half an hour. Shit, who could love a girl like her?"

Who?

Beauty is a hard thing. Beauty is a mean story. Beauty is slender girls who die young, fine-featured delicate creatures about whom men write poems. Beauty, my first girlfriend said to me, is that inner quality often associated with great amounts of leisure time. And I loved her for that.

We were not beautiful. We were hard and ugly and trying to be proud of it. The poor are plain, virtuous if humble and hardworking, but mostly ugly. Almost always ugly.

"You know Dot's husband left her," Cousin Billie told me once. "Came back after a while, then left again. Way she talked you'd think she never noticed. Some days I don't know whether to be proud of her or ashamed."

I thought about stories I'd been told, about women whose men left them or stayed to laugh out the sides of their mouths when other men mentioned other women's names. Behind my aunt Dot was a legion of female cousins and great-aunts, unknown and nameless—snuff-sucking, empty-faced creatures changing spindles at the textile plant, chewing gum while frying potatoes at the truck stop, exhausted, angry, and never loved enough.

The women I loved most in the world horrified me. I did not want to grow up to be them. I made myself proud of their pride, their determination, their stubbornness, but every night I prayed a man's prayer: Lord, save me from them. Do not let me become them.

Let me tell you the mean story.

For years and years, I convinced myself that I was unbreakable, an animal with an animal strength or something not human at all. Me, I told people, I take damage like a wall, a brick wall that never falls down, never feels anything, never flinches or re-members. I am one woman but I carry in my body all the stories I have ever been told, women I have known, women who have taken damage until they tell themselves they can feel no pain at all.

That's the mean story. That's the lie I told myself for years, and not until I began to fashion stories on the page did I sort it all out, see where the lie ended and a broken life remained. But that is not how I am supposed to tell it. I'm only supposed to tell one story at a time, one story. Every writing course I ever heard of said

the same thing. Take one story, follow it through, beginning, middle, end. I don't do that. I never do.

Behind the story I tell is the one I don't.

Behind the story you hear is the one I wish I could make you hear.

Behind my carefully buttoned collar is my nakedness, the struggle to find clean clothes, food, meaning, and money. Behind sex is rage, behind anger is love, behind this moment is silence, years of silence.

The man raped me. It's the truth. It's a fact.

I was five, and he was eight months married to my mother. That's how I always began to talk about it—when I finally did begin to talk about it.

I'd say, "It was rape, the rape of a child." Then I'd march the words out—all the old tearing awful words.

For years, every time I said it, said "rape" and "child" in the same terrible sentence, I would feel the muscles of my back and neck pull as taut as the string of a kite straining against the wind. That wind would blow and I would resist, then suddenly feel myself loosed to fall or flee. I started saying those words to get to that release, that feeling of letting go, of setting loose both the hatred and the fear. The need to tell my story was terrible and persistent, and I needed to say it bluntly and cruelly, to use all those words, those old awful tearing words.

I need to be a woman who can talk about rape plainly, without being hesitant or self-conscious, or vulnerable to what people might be saying this year.

I need to say that my mama didn't know what was going on, that I didn't tell her, that when I finally did tell someone it was not her. I need to say that when I told, only my mama believed me, only my mama did anything at all, that thirty years later one of my aunts could still say to me that she didn't really believe it, that he had been such a hardworking, good-looking man. Something else must have happened. Maybe it had been different.

How? I wanted to ask. How could it have been different for a five-year-old and a grown man? Instead I just looked at her, feeling finally strong enough to know she had chosen to believe what she needed more than what she knew.

Two or three things I know for sure, but none of them is why a man would rape a child, why a man would beat a child.

❧ WHY? I AM ASKED. Why do you bring that up? Must you talk about that? I asked myself the same questions until finally I began to understand. This was a wall in my life, I say, a wall I had to climb over every day. It was always there for me, deflecting my rage toward people who knew nothing about what had happened to me or why I should be angry at them.

It took me years to get past that rage, to say the words with grief and insistence but to let go of the anger, to refuse to use the anger against people who knew nothing of the rape. I had to learn how to say it, to say "rape," say "child," say "unending," "awful," and "relentless," and say it the way I do—

adamant, unafraid, unashamed, every time, all over again—to speak my words as a sacrament, a blessing, a prayer. Not a curse. Getting past the anger, getting to the release, I become someone else, and the story changes. I am no longer a grown-up outraged child but a woman letting go of her outrage, showing what I know: that evil is a man who imagines the damage he does is not damage, that evil is the act of pretending that some things do not happen or leave no mark if they do, that evil is not what remains when healing becomes possible.

All the things I can say about sexual abuse—about rape—none of them are reasons. The words do not explain. Explanations almost drove me crazy, other people's explanations and my own. Explanations, justifications, and theories. I've got my own theory. My theory is that rape goes on happening all the time. My theory is that everything said about that act is assumed to say something about me, as if that thing I never wanted to happen and did not know how to stop is the only thing that can be said about my life. My theory is that talking about it makes a difference—being a woman who can stand up anywhere and say, I was five and the man was big.

So let me say it.

He beat us, my stepfather, that short, mean-eyed truck driver with his tight-muscled shoulders and uneasy smile. He was a man who wasn't sure he liked women but was sure he didn't like smart, smart-mouthed tomboys, stubborn little girls who tried to pretend they were not afraid of him. Two or three things I know, but this is the one I am not supposed to talk about, how it comes together—sex and violence, love and hatred. I'm not ever supposed to put together the two halves of my life—the man who walked across my childhood and the life I have made for myself. I am not supposed to talk about hating that man when I grew up to be a lesbian, a dyke, stubborn, competitive, and perversely lustful.

"People might get confused," a woman once told me. She was a therapist and a socialist, but she worried about what people thought. "People might imagine that sexual abuse makes lesbians."

"Oh, I doubt it." I was too angry to be careful. "If it did, there would be so many more."

Her cheeks flushed pink and hot. She had told me once that she thought I didn't respect her—her oddly traditional life and commonplace desires, her husband of twelve years and female companion of five. Looking into her stern, uncompromising face brought back my aunts and their rueful certainty that nothing they did was ever quite right. Two or three things and none of them sure, that old voice whispered in my head while this woman looked at me out of eyes that had never squinted in regret.

"Tell me, though," I added, and shifted my shoulders like Aunt Dot leaning into a joke, "if people really believed that rape made lesbians, and brutal fathers made dykes, wouldn't they be more eager to do something about it? What's that old Marxist strategy—sharpen the contradiction until even the proletariat sees where the future lies? We could whack them with contradictions, use their bad instincts against their worse. Scare them into changing what they haven't even thought about before."

She opened her mouth like a fish caught on a razor-sharp line. For the first time in all the time I had known her I saw her genuinely enraged. She didn't think my suggestion was funny. But then, neither did I.

How *does* it come together, the sweaty power of violence, the sweet taste of desire held close? It rises in the simplest way, naturally and easily, when

you're so young you don't know what's coming, before you know why you're not supposed to talk
about it.

It came together for me when I was fifteen
and that man came after me with a belt for per-
haps the thousandth time and my little sister and
I did not run. Instead we grabbed up butcher
knives and backed him into a corner. And oh, the
way that felt! For once we made him sweat with
the threat of what we'd do if he touched us.
And oh! the joy of it, the power to say, "No, you
son of a bitch, this time, no!" His fear was sexual
and marvelous—hateful and scary but wonderful,
like orgasm, like waiting a whole lifetime and finally coming.

I know. I'm not supposed to talk about sex
like that, not about weapons or hatred or violence,
and never to put them in the context of sexual desire. Is it male? Is it mean? Did you get off on it?
I'm not supposed to talk about how good anger
can feel—righteous, justified, and completely sat-
isfying. Even at seventeen, when I learned to shoot
a rifle, I knew not to tell anyone what I saw and
felt as I aimed that weapon. Every time I centered
on the target it was his heart I saw, his squint-eyed,
mean-hearted image.

I knew that the things I was not sup-posed to say were also the things I did not want to think about. I knew the first time I made love with a woman that I could cry but I must not say why. I cried because she smelled like him, the memory of him, sweaty and urgent, and she must not know it was not her touch that made me cry. Breathing her in prompted in me both desire and hatred, and of the two feelings what I dared not think about was the desire. Sex with her be-came a part of throwing him off me, making peace with the violence of my own desire.

I know. I'm not supposed to talk about how long it took me to wash him out of my body—how many targets I shot, how many women I slept with, how many times I sat up till dawn wondering if it would ever change, if I would ever change. If there would come a time in my life when desire did not resonate with fury.

Two or three things I know for sure, and one of them is that change when it comes cracks everything open.

🌿 LET ME TELL YOU A STORY. Let me tell you the story that is in no part fiction, the story of the female body taught to hate itself.

It is so hard to be a girl and want what you have never had. To be a child and want what you cannot imagine. To look at women and think, Nobody else, nobody else has ever wanted to do what I want to do. Hard to be innocent, believing yourself evil. Hard to think no one else in the history of the world wants to do this. Hard to find out that they do, but not with you. Or not in quite the way you want them to do it.

Women.

Lord God, I used to follow these girls.

They would come at me, those girls who were not really girls anymore. Grown up, wounded, hurt and terrible. Pained and desperate. Mean and angry. Hungry and unable to say just what they needed. Scared, aching, they came into my bed like I could fix it. And every time I would try. I would do anything a woman wanted as long as she didn't want too much of me. As long as I could hide behind her need, I could make her believe anything. I would tell her stories. I would bury her in them. I have buried more women than I am willing to admit. I have told more lies than I can stand.

I never thought about what I needed, how hurt and desperate I was, how mean and angry and dangerous. When I finally saw it, the grief I had been hiding even from myself, the world seemed to stop while I looked. For a year, then another, I kept myself safe, away from anyone, any feeling that might prompt that rage, that screaming need to hurt somebody back.

When I finally let someone into my narrow bed, the first thing I told her was what I could not do. I said, "I can't fix it, girl. I can't fix anything. If you don't ask me to fix it, you can ask anything else. If you can say what you need, I'll try to give it to you."

I remember the stories I was told as a girl, stories like soap operas, stories that went on for generations—how she loved him and left him and loved him still, how he hurt her and hurt her and never loved her at all, how that child they made told lies to get them to look at her, how no one knows the things done in that home, no one but her and she don't tell.

Women lose their lives not knowing they can do something different. Men eat themselves up believing they have to be the thing they have been made. Children go crazy. Really, even children go crazy, believing the shape of the life they must live is as small and mean and broken as they are told. Oh, I could tell you stories that would darken the sky and stop the blood. The stories I could tell no one would believe. I would have to pour blood on the floor to convince anyone that every word I say is true. And then? Whose blood would speak for me?

Let me tell you a story. I tell stories to prove I was meant to survive, knowing it is not true. My stories are no parables, no *Reader's Digest* Unforgettable Characters, no women's movement polemics, no Queer Nation broadsides. I am not here to make anyone happy. What I am here for is to claim my life, my mama's death, our losses and our triumphs, to name them for myself. I am here to claim everything I know, and there are only two or three things I know for sure.

"How'd you know you were a lesbian?"

My sister Wanda was eighteen when she finally asked me that question. We were sitting on the steps of the feminist collective where I was living in Tallahassee, Florida. It was her matter-of-fact tone that surprised me, that and the direct way she put the question. From the moment she climbed off the bus with her hair tied back in braids, I had been talking to her about feminism, the women's center, and the child-care center where I was a volunteer every Sunday afternoon. I wondered what had prompted the question— maybe one of our posters or the way my housemates congregated around the pool table that dominated what was supposed to be our dining room. I wondered if I should give her the stock answer, right out of the radical women's newsletters on my nightstand: that I became a lesbian because of my commitment to a women's revolution.

I looked into her deceptively clear brown eyes

and considered the question. I pushed my hair behind my ears. "I fell in love with a woman," I said, matching her in tone and attitude. Her mouth quirked, one side twitching as if she wanted to grin but didn't dare.

"Well," she drawled, and looked away as if that would help her not to laugh, "that'll do it, I suppose. Almost surely."

I rescued her by letting myself giggle. She joined me. I reminded myself that there were just some things we never had talked about before, like sex, money, and broken bones. Certainly we had never discussed love. Sex was dangerous enough, and our family was proof that love was a disaster waiting to happen.

"The woman love you back?" Wanda asked me. "She treat you good?"

"No." I said it again. "No. She was like that boy you wanted to marry. She treated me just about like he treated you. Took me a long time to grow up and stop falling in love with women who would treat me bad." I said it as if it were accomplished, as if I were not at that moment in love with yet another hard-eyed bitter woman.

Wanda nodded but didn't look at me, just sat there twisting the ring on her middle finger and staring into the parking lot across the street.

"Yeah," she whispered. "Takes a damn long time to learn that, don't it?"

Women talk about sex in such strange ways— carefully, obliquely, cautiously, almost shamefully. The art of flirting is an art of indirection. The dance is deliberately extended; eyes meet and slide away, limbs barely touch, erotic messages are communicated by the most subtle gestures. It brings out in me the most profound feelings of anxiety and exasperation. I was not raised to subtlety.

Why do people have to make such a fuss over something so simple?

I say, "Talk to me. Tell me who you are, what you want, what you've never had, the story you've always been afraid to tell." Women stare at me, blush, squirm—and now and then, a few gather up their courage and flirt back.

But flirting is an art form, separate entirely from the risks and surprises of love, and to love I had thought myself immune. Because I did not turn silly at thirteen, start staying out late and sighing over boys at school, I thought myself too smart, too wise, too special to fall into the trap every other woman in my family knew too well. I watched my cousins mourn over their swollen bellies, wipe puffy eyes and talk bitterly about the boys who had used them so badly, and all I could think was how foolish the whole thing was.

Love was something I would not have to worry about—the whole mystery of love, heartbreak songs, and family legends. Women who pined, men who went mad, people who forgot who they were and shamed themselves with need, wanting only to be loved by the one they loved. Love was a mystery. Love was a calamity. Love was a curse that had somehow skipped me, which was no doubt why I was so good at multiple-choice tests and memorizing poetry. Sex was the country I had been dragged into as an unwilling girl—sex, and the madness of the body. For all that it could terrify and confuse me, sex was something I had assimilated. Sex was a game or a weapon or an addiction. Sex was familiar. But love—love was another country.

"Lord!" I shouted. "There has got to be an easier way to get stoned."

I was staying over at my friend Pat's house, sitting on the floor leaning against the stereo speakers, which had been blasting rock and roll at maximum volume just moments before. We had been using a process a friend had suggested, a three-step method that began with smoking rabbit weed we'd harvested from the border of the Maynard Evans High School parking lot, then running in place very fast, and then putting our heads between two stereo speakers propped ten inches apart.

"Sure there is." Pat leaned over and slapped my hip. "First we take a bus to New York City, find us Washington Square Park like in that book you got, flirt with some dangerous-looking people until they decide we an't dogmeat, and maybe then we get them to sell us some real marijahootchi. That sound easier to you?"

"Less likely to cause nausea, anyway."

"I don't know. I like this." Pat shook her head as if the roar were still echoing in her skull. "It's like my head is swinging free from my neck. Maybe this is as good as it gets."

"I don't think so." I sat up and watched her swing her head. Pat had cut her thick brown hair short again so that it just curved under her ears. Her neck looked remarkably smooth and sweet under the sweep of those curls. Some days Pat wanted to grow up to be the modern incarnation of T. E. Lawrence, others she dreamed of becoming a balladeer like Judy Collins or Joan Baez. To prepare, we drank bitter coffee and wrote lyrics together, long terrible poems about death.

"You know, I been thinking about going." Pat looked at me from between the fringes of her bangs. "Thinking about dumping school completely and running off. Find me some real dope and people who an't planning on working at the Winn Dixie the rest of their lives."

It was a conversation we had had dozens of times. We'd talked about running off until we knew just how to go about it. We'd memorize the bus fares for all the cities we were considering, and played at making up false IDs. Sometimes it was only the game that kept us from actually buying that Trailways ticket out of town. This time should have been no different from any other. I should have chimed in with my own curses, said, "Damn yes, let's go."

But I did not. There was something in Pat's voice, some edge of frustration. Her eyes were turned away, but I could see just how dark and bright they had become. She's going to do it, I thought, and shocked myself with a wave of desperate longing. The rush of my need stunned me—not to go with her but to keep her with me. Suddenly I understood that more than anything in the world I did not want Pat to disappear out of my life into some strange Yankee city, some alien life where I could not follow. My mouth opened, and I barely stopped myself from begging her to stay.

I looked down and saw my own body as a hated stranger might see it. I looked up and saw Pat's eyes looking back at me—unafraid, dispassionate, curious. She had no way of knowing that without warning or preparation I had just become my mother's daughter, my sisters' counterpart—tender and fragile and hungry for something besides dispassionate curiosity. This was what everyone had known that I had not, this sudden onslaught of desire and terror.

"I got to go," I told her, and headed for the door. I did not look back, afraid she might see what I knew was on my face.

Three months later Pat was gone, running north with a vanload of friends I didn't know. It would be a decade before I saw her again on her mother's porch, her hair cut shorter still, her mouth loose with Valium, both arms in casts acquired when she had thrown herself out of a moving car.

"You ever get to Washington Square Park?" she asked me.

"Yeah."

"Wasn't what I thought it would be. Ratty place full of ratty people." Her words were slurred. Her eyes tracked away from me.

I curled my fingernails into my palms. I couldn't think of anything to say, certainly not "I'm sorry" or "I think I loved you."

"Well, hell!" For a moment I saw an old spark in Pat's eyes. "You come back when I get these damn casts off. I been writing some poems will give you a headache just to be in the room with them." She grinned, and I knew I loved her still.

At twenty-four I joined a karate class and learned for the first time how to run without fear pushing me. It was not what I had intended. I never ex-

pected to join the class at all. I showed up because I had been told there were no women allowed and my newfound feminist convictions insisted someone had to do something about that. Along with my friend Flo, I dressed in loose clothes and hitched a ride out to the university gardens very early one Monday morning.

On a rutted dirt lane a small group of peevish-looking young males were climbing out of rusty old cars and pulling off shoes.

"Where's the sensei?" I demanded of one of those boys. He stared at me blankly. I stared right back and repeated my question.

That boy just stood there, looking from me to Flo to his friends. Then somebody laughed. Flo and I glared fiercely. One of the boys stepped forward and gave me a nod.

"Down there," he said. "A quarter mile down that path. The class is out there where the teacher's waiting." Then he nodded again and took off in an easy lope. The other boys stepped around us and followed.

I watched their bare feet pick up fine dust and kick it into the cool, moist grass along the path. Without thought, Flo and I fell in behind them. It was a long, winding run down into a hollow and then up around a wide grassy hill. My thighs and calves started to ache in the first thirty feet. Only stubbornness kept me moving, following those boys, who would occasionally look back and snicker. Later I would be grateful for their laughter. Without it, I would never have managed the full quarter mile, especially not the last curving uphill grade to where a soft-featured, blond young man was doing some kind of stylized kicking exercise.

The sensei stopped to watch us stagger up the hill. The boys were ahead of us, and I couldn't hear what they told him, but his first words were as precise as his motions.

"You want to join the class, you'll have to do better than that."

"We will," I announced emphatically, trying not to gasp for air. The sensei just nodded and started the class, putting Flo and me at the back as if suddenly adding two women to his all-male domain were something he had hoped to do all along—which it was, though we knew nothing of that.

The first weeks we kept coming just to hear the sensei tell us we could not come back. But every day he welcomed us as he welcomed the boys, requiring that we first complete that run, then stand silent, breathing as he breathed, deep and slow, trying to feel each muscle in hips and shoulders and neck. I barely heard him. For me those weeks were grim agony. I was making demands on muscles I had ignored most of my life, and only because I expected the ordeal to be over soon.

The boys helped. Every time they laughed, I would make myself stand taller or move faster. Every time they looked back over their shoulders at my stumbling attempts at running, I would grit my teeth and force my legs to pump higher. So long as they laughed, I would not quit. So long as they watched for tears, I would not let myself cry, though some days to cry was what I wanted most to do—to lie down in the damp grass and weep at the inept female body in which I was imprisoned.

Two, three, four weeks, we kept going. The laughter eased off, but not my desire to cry. Was it in the fourth week or the fifth that the teacher brought his wife to class? A ballet dancer with long, long legs, she easily outdistanced all of us on tight-muscled calves. Nothing daunted that woman, not the run or the kicking or even lifting one of those big pink-faced boys to her shoulders and showing us how to step in a gracefully wide stance while holding him easily. I watched her in confusion, understanding completely what was intended, the example of that astonishingly perfected female body taking over the class and showing us all what a woman could do. I watched the sensei watching her and understood that not only would he not ask us to leave his class but that the passion in his glance was something rare and unknown to me: love that yearned as much for the spirit as for the body.

I looked at her then as he looked at her, and

somehow she became a story in my head, a memory of a woman I had seen once dancing on the balls of her feet, arms moving like scythes, face stern, eyes alive. Naked and powerful, deadly and utterly at peace with herself. She had a body that had never forgotten itself, and I knew at once that what I was seeing was magic. Watching, I fell in love—not with her but with the body itself, the hope of movement, the power of jumping and thrusting and being the creature that is not afraid to fall down but somehow doesn't anyway.

Running the quarter mile back from that class, I started to cry. I made no sound, no gesture, just kept moving and letting the teardrops sheet down my face. Everyone was way ahead of me. My hands were curled into fists, pumping at my sides. The tears became sobs, heartbroken and angry, and I stumbled, almost falling down before I caught my footing in a different gait. My hips shifted. Something in the bottom of my spine let go. Something disconnected from the coccyx that was shattered when I was a girl. Something loosened from the old bruised and torn flesh. Some piece of shame pulled free, some shame so ancient I had never known myself without it. I felt it lift, and with it my thighs lifted, suddenly loose and strong, pumping steadily beneath me as if nothing could hold me down.

I picked up speed and closed in on the boys ahead of me, Flo there among them like a female gazelle. I saw her head turn and discover me running just behind her. She ignored my wet face and produced a welcoming grin, then stepped aside so that we were running together, elbow to elbow, her legs setting a pace for mine. I breathed deep and felt the muscles in my neck open, something strong getting stronger. If there was love in the world, I thought, then there was no reason I should not have it in my life. I matched Flo's pace and kept running.

I fell in love with karate though I remained a white belt, year after year of white belts—a legendary white belt, in fact. I was so bad, people would come to watch. Inflexible, nearsighted, without talent or aptitude, falling down, sweaty and miserable—sometimes I would even pass out halfway through the class. I learned to take a glass of bouillon like medicine before I put on my gi. But I kept going back, careless of injury or laughter. What I wanted from karate was some echo of love for my body and the spirit it houses—meat and bone and the liquid song of my own gasps, the liquor stink of stubborn sweat, the sweet burn of sinew, muscle, and lust.

I studied karate for eight years, going from school to school, city to city, always starting over. My first sensei was the best I ever found. That moment of perfect physical consciousness was more often memory than reality. I did not become suddenly coordinated, develop perfect vision in my near-blind right eye, or turn jock and take up half a dozen sports. All I gained was a sense of what I might do, could do if I worked at it, a sense of my body as my own. And that was miracle enough.

She kissed me gentle, kissed me slow, kissed me like Grace Kelly, a porcelain princess, a lace-curtain lesbian.

I told her, Don't touch me that way. Don't come at me with that sour-cream smile. Come at me as if I were worth your life—the life we make together. Take me like a turtle whose shell must be cracked, whose heart is ice, who needs your heat. Love me like a warrior, sweat up to your earlobes and all your hope between your teeth. Love me so I know I am at least as important as anything you have ever wanted.

I am the woman who lost herself but now is

found, the lesbian, outside the law of church and man, the one who has to love herself or die. If you are not as strong as I am, what will we make together? I am all muscle and wounded desire, and I need to know how strong we both can be.

Two or three things I know for sure, and one of them is how long it takes to learn to love yourself, how long it took me, how much love I need now.

THE LAST TIME MY STEPFATHER BEAT ME, I was sixteen years old. It was my birthday, and he got away with it because he pretended that what he was doing was giving me a birthday spanking, a tradition in our family as in so many others. But two of my girlfriends were standing there, and even they could see he was hitting me harder than any birthday ritual could justify. I saw their faces go pink with embarrassment. I knew mine was hot with shame, but I could not stop him or pull free of him. The moment stretched out while his hand crashed down, counting off each year of my life. At sixteen, I jumped free and turned to face him.

"You can't break me," I told him. "And you're never going to touch me again."

It was a story to tell myself, a promise. Saying out loud, "You're never going to touch me again"—that was a piece of magic, magic in the belly, the domed kingdom of sex, the terror place inside where rage and power live. Whiskey rush without whiskey, bravado and determination, this place where for the first time I knew no confusion, only outrage and pride. In the worst moments of my life, I have told myself that story, the story about a girl who stood up to a monster. Doing that, I make a piece of magic inside myself, magic to use against the meanness in the world.

I know. I am supposed to have shrunk down

and died. I know. I am supposed to be deeply broken, incapable of love or trust or passion. But I am not, and part of why that is so is the nature of the stories I told myself to survive. Like the stories my mama told herself, and my aunt Dot and my cousin Billie, my stories shaped my life. Of all the stories I know, the meanest are the stories the women I loved told themselves in secret—the stories that sustained and broke them.

When I make love I take my whole life in my hands, the damage and the pride, the bad memories and the good, all that I am or might be, and I do indeed love myself, can indeed do any damn thing I please. I know the place where courage and desire come together, where pride and joy push lust through the bloodstream, right to the heart.

I go to bed like I used to go to karate. Want and need come together in a body that is only partly my own. Like my sisters, like my mama, I am and am not this thing the world sees—strong chin, hard eyes, a mouth too soft when it should be firm, a creature of lust who does not know how to feel what I feel. Biblical? Damned? Hopeful. What is lust when you have never known love?

I took my sex back, my body. I claimed myself and remade my life. Only when I knew I belonged to myself completely did I become capable of giving myself to another, of finding joy in desire, pleasure in our love, power in this body no one else owns.

I am the only one who can tell the story of my life and say what it means. I knew that as a child. It was one of the reasons not to tell. When I finally got away, left home and looked back, I thought it was like that story in the Bible, that incest is a coat of many colors, some of them not visible to the human eye, but so vibrant, so powerful, people looking at you wearing it see only the coat. I did not want to wear that coat, to be told

what it meant, to be told how it had changed the flesh beneath it, to let myself be made over into my rapist's creation. I will not wear that coat, not even if it is recut to a feminist pattern, a postmodern analysis.

Two or three things I know for sure, and one is that I would rather go naked than wear the coat the world has made for me.

🍂 WHAT IS THE STORY I WILL NOT TELL? The story I do not tell is the only one that is a lie. It is the story of the life I do not lead, without complication, mystery, courage, or the transfiguration of the flesh. Yes, somewhere inside me there is a child always eleven years old, a girlchild who holds the world responsible for all the things that terrify and call to me. But inside me too is the teenager who armed herself and fought back, the dyke who did what she had to, the woman who learned to love without giving in to fear. The stories other people would tell about my life, my mother's life, my sisters', uncles', cousins', and lost girlfriends'—those are the stories that could destroy me, erase me, mock and deny me. I tell my stories louder all the time: mean and ugly stories; funny, almost bitter stories; passionate, desperate stories—all of them have to be told in order not to tell the one the world wants, the story of us broken, the story of us never laughing out loud, never learning to enjoy sex, never being able to love or trust love again, the story in which all that survives is the flesh. That is not my story. I tell all the others so as not to have to tell that one.

Two or three things I know, two or three things I know for sure, and one of them is that to go on living I have to tell stories, that stories are the one sure way I know to touch the heart and change the world.

I HAD THIS GIRLFRIEND once scared all my other girlfriends off. Big, blond, shy, and butch, just out of the army, drove a two-door Chevy with a reinforced trunk and wouldn't say why.

"What you carry in that thing, girl? You moving contraband state to state?" I was joking, teasing, putting my hand on her butt, grinning at her scowl, touching her in places she couldn't quite admit she liked.

"I an't moving nothing," she told me.

"Uh-huh. Right. So how come I feel so moved?"

She blushed. I love it when women blush, especially those big butch girls who know you want them. And I wanted her. I did. I wanted her. But she was a difficult woman, wouldn't let me give her a backrub, read her palm, or sew up the tear in her jeans—all those ritual techniques Southern femmes have employed in the seduction of innocent butch girls. A basic error, this one was not from the South. Born in Chicago, she was a Yankee runaway raised in Barbados by a daddy who worked as a Mafia bagman and was never really sure if he was bringing up a boy or a girl. He'd bought her her first three-piece suit, then cursed at how good it looked on her and signed the permission form that let her join the army at seventeen.

"My daddy loves me, he just don't understand me. Don't know how to talk to me when I go back." She told me that after I'd helped her move furniture for two hours and we were relaxing over a shared can of beer and stories of how she'd gotten to Tallahassee. I just nodded, pretty sure her daddy understood her as much as he could stand.

I seduced her in the shower. It was all that

furniture-moving, I told her, and insisted I couldn't go out in the condition I was in. Simple courtesy. I sent her in the shower first, came in after, and then soaped her back in businesslike fashion so she'd relax a little more. I kept chatting—about the women's center, books I'd read, music, and oh! how long and thick her toenails were. I got down on my knees to examine her toenails.

"Woman," I said, "you have the most beautiful feet."

I let the water pour down over both of us. It was a silly thing, to talk that way in that situation, but sex is like that. There I was, kneeling for her, naked, my hands on her legs, my mouth just where I wanted it to be. I smiled before I leaned forward. She clenched her fists in my hair, moaned when my tongue touched her. The muscles in her thighs began to jump. We nearly drowned in that shower.

"Don't laugh at me," she said later when we were lying limp on wet sheets, and I promised. No.

"Whiskey and cigarettes," she mumbled. "I move whiskey and cigarettes without tax stamps, for the money, that's what I move."

I smiled and raked my teeth across her throat. "Uh-huh."

"And . . ." She paused. I put one leg between

her thighs and slid myself up and down until we fit tight, the bone of my hip resting against the arch of her pubic mound, the tangle of her blond curls wiry on my belly. I pushed up off her throat and waited. She looked up at me. Her cheeks were bright red, her eyes almost closed, pearly tears showing at the corners.

"Shaklee! Shaklee products. Oh God! I sell cleaning supplies door to door."

I bit her shoulder, didn't laugh. I rocked her on my leg until she relaxed and laughed herself. I rocked her until she could forgive me for asking. Then she took hold of me and rolled me over and showed me that she wanted me as much as I had wanted her.

"You're quite a story," I whispered to her after.

"Don't tell," she begged.

"Who would I tell?"

Who needs to know?

Not until I was thirty-four did my sister Anne and I sit down together to talk about our lives. She came out on the porch, put a six-pack on my lap, and gave me a wary careful grin.

"All right," Anne said. "You drink half the six-pack and then we'll talk."

"I can't drink," I said.

"I know." She grinned at me.

I frowned. Then, very deliberately, I pulled one of the cans free from the plastic loop, popped it open, and drank deeply. The beer wasn't as cold as it should have been, but the taste was sweet and familiar.

"Not bad," I complimented Anne.

"Yeah, I gave up on those fifty-nine-cent

bargains. These days I spend three dollars or I don't buy."

"I'm impressed."

"Oh, don't start. You've never been impressed with anything I've done or said or thought of doing. You were so stuck up you never noticed me at all."

"I noticed." I looked at her, remembering her at thirteen—the first time she had accused me of being weird, making fun of me for not wearing makeup or even knowing what kind of clothes I should have been begging Mama to buy me. "You don't do nothing but read, do you?" Her words put her in the hated camp of my stepfather, who was always snatching books out of my hands and running me out of the house.

"We didn't like each other much," Anne said.

"We didn't know each other."

"Yeah? Well, Mama always thought you peed rose water."

"But you were beautiful. Hell, you didn't even have to pee, you were so pretty. People probably offered to pee for you."

"Oh, they offered to do something, right enough." She gave me a bitter smile.

"You made me feel so ugly."

"You made me feel so stupid."

I couldn't make a joke out of that. Instead, I tried to get her to look at me. I reached over and put my hand on her arm.

When we were girls, my little sister Anne had light shiny hair, fine skin, and guileless eyes. She was a girl whose walk at twelve made men stop to watch her pass, a woman at thirteen who made grown men murderous and teenage boys sweaty with hunger. My mother watched her with the fear of a woman who had been a beautiful girl. I watched her with painful jealousy. Why was she so pretty when I was so plain? When strangers in the grocery store smiled at her and complimented Mama on "that lovely child," I glared and turned away. I wanted to be what my little sister was. I wanted all the things that appeared to be possible for her.

It took me years to learn the truth behind that lie. It took my sister two decades to tell me what it was really like being beautiful, about the hatred that trailed over her skin like honey melting on warm bread.

My beautiful sister had been dogged by contempt just like her less beautiful sisters—more, for she dared to be different yet again, to hope when she was supposed to have given up hope, to dream when she was not the one they saved dreams for. Her days were full of boys sneaking over to pinch her breasts and whisper threats into her ears, of girls who warned her away from their brothers, of thin-lipped adults who lost no opportunity to tell her she really didn't know how to dress.

"You think you pretty, girl? Ha! You an't nothing but another piece of dirt masquerading as better."

"You think you something? What you thinking, you silly bitch?"

I think she was beautiful. I think she still is.

My little sister learned the worth of beauty. She dropped out of high school and fell in love with a boy who got a bunch of his friends to swear that the baby she was carrying could just as easily have been theirs as his. By eighteen she was no longer beautiful, she was ashamed: staying up nights with her bastard son, living in my stepfather's house, a dispatcher for a rug company, unable to afford her own place, desperate to give her life to the first man who would treat her gently.

"Sex ruined that girl," I heard a neighbor tell my mama. "Shoulda kept her legs closed, shoulda known what would happen to her."

"You weren't stupid," I said, my hand on Anne's arm, my words just slightly slurred.

"Uh-huh. Well, you weren't ugly."

We popped open more cans and sat back in our chairs. She talked about her babies. I told her about my lovers. She cursed the men who had hurt her. I told her terrible stories about all the mean women who had lured me into their beds when it wasn't me they really wanted. She told me she had always hated the sight of her husband's cock. I told her that sometimes, all these years later, I still wake up crying, not sure what I have dreamed about, but remembering something bad and crying like a child in great pain. She got a funny look on her face.

"I made sure you were the one," she said. "The one who had to take him his glasses of tea, anything at all he wanted. And I hated myself for it. I knew every time, when you didn't come right back—I knew he was keeping you in there, next to him, where you didn't want to be any more than I did."

She looked at me, then away. "But I never really knew what he was doing," she whispered. "I thought you were so strong. Not like me. I knew I wasn't strong at all. I thought you were like Mama, that you could handle him. I thought you could handle anything. Every time he'd grab hold of me and hang on too long, he'd make me feel so bad and frightened and unable to imagine what he wanted, but afraid, so afraid. I didn't think you felt like that. I didn't think it was the same for you."

We were quiet for a while, and then my sister leaned over and pressed her forehead to my cheek.

"It wasn't fair, was it?" she whispered.

"None of it was," I whispered back, and put my arms around her.

"Goddamn!" she cursed. "Goddamn!" And started to cry. Just that fast, I was crying with her.

"But Mama really loved you, you know," Anne said.

"But you were beautiful."

She put her hands up to her cheeks, to the fine webs of wrinkles under her eyes, the bruised shadows beneath the lines. The skin of her upper arms hung loose and pale. Her makeup ended in a ragged line at her neck, and below it, the skin was puckered, freckled, and sallow.

I put my hand on her head, on the full blond mane that had been her glory when she was twelve. Now she was thirty-two, and the black roots showing at her scalp were sprinkled with gray. I pulled her to me, hugged her, and kissed her neck. Slowly we quieted our crying, holding on to each other. Past my sister's shoulder, I saw her girl coming toward us, a chubby dark child with nervous eyes.

"Mama. Mama, y'all all right?"

My sister turned to her daughter. For a moment I thought she was going to start crying again, but instead she sighed. "Baby," she called, and she put her hands out to touch those little-girl porcelain cheeks. "Oh baby, you know how your mama gets."

"You know how your mama gets." The words echoed in me. If I closed my eyes, I could see again the yellow kitchens of our childhood, where Mama hung her flowered curtains every time we moved, as if they were not cotton but spirit. It was as if every move were another chance to begin again, to claim some safe and clean space for herself and her girls. Every time, we watched her, thinking this time maybe it would be different. And when different did not come, when, every time, the same nightmarish scenes unfolded—shouting and crying and Mama sitting hopelessly at her kitchen table—she spoke those words.

"Oh, girls, you know how your mama gets."

I clenched my hands on my thighs, seeing my niece's mouth go hard. She clamped her teeth as I remembered clamping mine, looked away as I would have done, not wanting to see two tired, half-drunk women looking back at her with her own features. I shook my head once and caught her glance, the wise and sullen look of a not quite adolescent girl who knew too much.

"Pretty girl," I said. "Don't look so hard."

Her mouth softened slightly. She liked being told she was pretty. At eleven so had I. I waved her to my hip, and when she came, I pushed her hair back off her face, using the gestures my mama had used on me. "Oh, you're going to be something special," I told her. Something special.

"My baby's so pretty," Anne said. "Look at her. My baby's just the most beautiful thing in the whole wide world." She grinned, and shook her head. "Just like her mama, huh?" Her voice was only a little bitter, only a little cruel. Just like her mama.

I looked into my niece's sunburned frightened face. Like her mama, like her grandmama, like her aunts—she had that hungry desperate look that trusts nothing and wants everything. She didn't think she was pretty. She didn't think she was worth anything at all.

"Let me tell you a story," I whispered. "Let me tell you a story you haven't heard yet." Oh, I wanted to take her, steal her, run with her a thousand miles away from the daddy who barely noticed her, the men who had tried to do to her what my stepfather had done to me. I wanted to pick her up and cradle her. I wanted to save her.

My niece turned her face to me, open and trusting, waiting to be taken away, to be persuaded, or healed, or simply distracted.

All right, I thought. That will do. For one moment, this moment leading to the next, the act of storytelling connecting to the life that might be possible, I held her attention and began.

"Let me tell you about your mama."

My niece looked from me to my sister, and my sister stared at me uncertainly, wondering if I was going to hurt her, her and her girl.

"Sit down, baby. I got a story to tell you. Look at your mama. You know how she is? Well, let me tell you about the day death was calling your mama's name, death was singing her song and luring her away. She was alone, as alone as only a woman waiting to birth a baby can be. All she saw was darkness. All she heard was her blood singing death. But in the deepest part of that night she heard something else. She heard the baby in her belly crying soft, too weak to make a big noise, too small to know it was alive at all. That's when your mama saved her own life—by choosing it, by claiming it, alone and scared as she was. By pulling you into the world and loving you with her whole heart."

I watched my sister's eyes go wide, watched her mouth work. "Now you telling stories about me?"

I just smiled. "Oh, I got one or two."

That night I sat with my niece and watched my sister going in and out her back door, picking up and sweeping, scolding her dogs for jumping up on her clean work clothes. My niece was sleepy, my sister exhausted. Their features were puffy, pale, and too much alike. I surprised myself then, turning my niece's face to mine and starting another story.

"When your mama was a girl," I told her, "she was so beautiful people said the sun shone brighter when she walked out in the day. They said the moon took on glitter when she went out in the night. But, strangest of all, people said the June bugs catching sight of her would begin to light and try to sing an almost human song. It got to the point she had to stay home and hide to keep the sun from getting too hot, the moon from burning up, the June bugs from going hoarse and dying out."

"Ahhh." The two of them looked at me, almost smiling, almost laughing, waiting. I put my hand out, not quite touching my sister's face, and drew my fingers along the line of her neck from just below her ear to the softness of her chin. With my other hand I made the same gesture along my niece's face.

"See here?" I whispered. "This is where you can see it. That's the mark of the beautiful Gibson women, both of you have it."

My niece touched her cheek, mouth open.

"Here?" she asked.

Yes.

Two or three things I know, two or three things I know for sure, and one of them is that if we are not beautiful to each other, we cannot know beauty in any form.

TEN DAYS AFTER MY SON, Wolf, was born, my sister Wanda came to stay with us. "Gonna make sure you know what you're doing," she'd joked before she came. "Waiting till you're forty-two to start a family, what you think? You think it's as easy as reading a book? You think it comes natural, raising babies and not going crazy? Lord!"

I didn't argue. I put Wolf in her arms and let her pull his belly up to her chin, let her tickle his ears and kiss his neck.

"I thought boys would be different," she told me. "But he smells like my girls."

She grinned and licked his cheek. "Tastes like them, too." Wolf giggled and I laughed with him, and only then saw that there were tears on Wanda's eyelashes.

"Babies!" she teased. "Get you every time."

Later she told me she'd only come to save herself another pregnancy. "Got to where I'd started dreaming about having another one, breathing in that talcum smell, feeling those little arms hanging on my neck." She sipped at a beer and grinned at me over Wolf's extended fingers.

I waved a diaper at her and laughed. "Wasn't it you that told me mamas go crazy from sleep deprivation?"

"Oh yeah. Sleep deprivation, sex deprivation, and the simple lack of adult conversation. Drive you out of your head in a matter of weeks. Make you act silly when it an't making you think you dreaming all the time." She cradled Wolf's bare feet in one hand as if she wanted to lick them the way she'd licked his cheek.

"Used to think people were talking to me when there was nobody else there."

"Yeah," I agreed. "The other night I even thought I heard Mama, just outside the window, talking to someone else."

Wanda's eyes turned up from Wolf's toes to my face. "Might have been, you know."

"I don't believe that."

"Just the same. Might have been. Babies change things, open doors you thought were shut, close others. Make you into something you never been. You the mama now, you're gonna think different. Hell, you'll be different after a while, all the time more than what you thought you were. Or maybe a little less."

I gave her a careful look. Asked, "You get religion again when I wasn't looking?" And waited to see if she'd joke her way out of saying more.

For a moment she was quiet, her fingers gently stroking my boy's feet, her eyes still looking into mine.

"Nothing's different and everything's changed. That's all. You've moved to California and got yourself a baby. I'm an old married woman with two half-grown girls of my own. When did we think this was gonna happen to either of us, huh? When did we believe we were gonna live this long?"

"Two or three things and nothing for sure, huh?"

"Yeah." And she kissed Wolf's head.

More than a decade ago I had to quit karate. My body broke in a way that stubbornness could not heal. The notched indexes of my vertebrae, separated only by the thinnest cushioned lining, met and grated loud enough to echo in my nervous system.

These days I go to strange places, cities I've never been, stand up in public, in front of strangers, assume the position, open my mouth, and tell stories.

It is not an act of war.

Two or three things I know for sure and one of them is that telling the story all the way through is an act of love.

❧ OTHER NIGHT I WENT over to Providence to read in a line, a marathon of poets and fiction writers.

Afterwards, as I was sipping a Coke, a young man came up to me, fierce and tall and skinny, his wrists sticking out of his sleeves.

He said, "Hypertext. I've been wanting to tell you about it."

"Hypertext?"

"Your work. I've read everything you've ever published three or four times—at least. I know your work. I could put you in hypertext."

There was a girl behind him. She reached past his sleeve, put her hand on mine, said, "Oh yes, we could do it. We could put you in hypertext." She spoke the word with conviction, passion, almost love.

"Hypertext?" I spoke it through a blur of bewilderment.

"CD-ROM, computers, disks or files, it doesn't matter," the boy said in a rush of intensity. "It's the latest thing. We take one of your stories, and we put you in. I know just the story. It goes all the way through from beginning to end. But all the way through, people can reach in and touch a word. Mouse or keyboard or a touchable screen. Every time you touch a word, a window opens. Behind that word is another story. You touch the word and the story opens. We put one of your stories behind that story. And then maybe, maybe you could write some more and we could put in other things. Every word the reader touches, it opens again."

The girl tugged my arm urgently. "It's so beautiful," she said. "After a while it's like a skin of oil on the water. If you look at it from above it's just one thing, water and oil in a spreading shape. But if you looked at it from the side, it would go down and down, layers and layers. All the stories you've ever told. All the pictures you've ever seen. We can put in everything. Hypertext."

The boy nodded.

I reached for a glass of wine. I took a long drink, rubbed my aching back, said, "Yeah, right, I'll think about it."

That night I had a dream.

I was walking in a museum, and I was old. I was on that cane I had to use the whole length of 1987. My right eye had finally gone completely blind. My left eye was tearing steadily. I saw everything through a scrim of water, oily water. Way way down three or four corridors, around a turn, I hit a wall.

My story was on this wall.

I stood in front of my wall. I put my hand on it. Words were peeling across the wall, and every word was a brick. I touched one.

"Bastard."

The brick fell away and a window opened. My mother was standing in front of me. She was saying, "I'm not sick. I would tell you if I was sick, girl. I would tell you."

I touched her face and the window opened.

She was behind it, flesh cooling, still warm. Hair gone, shadows under her eyes. I was crying. I touched her hand. It was marble, it was brick. It fell away. She was seventeen and she was standing on the porch. He was sitting on the steps. She was smiling at him. She was saying, "You won't treat me bad, will you? You'll love my girls, won't you?"

I touched the brick. It fell away.

He was standing there. I was holding my arm. The doctor was saying, "What in God's name happened to this child?"

I touched the wall and the brick fell away.

My mama had her hand on my neck. She was handing me pictures. She was saying, "I didn't want to know who they were. I don't know what happened. I never wanted to tell you what happened. You make it up for yourself."

I put my hand on the photograph and the window opened onto a movie. I was eight years old. Cousins and aunts and strangers were moving across the yard. I was clinging to my mother's neck. I was saying "Mama" in that long, low plea a frightened child makes.

She reached for me, put her arms around me. I fell away. She was holding onto her mama's neck, saying the same thing, saying "Mama" in that same cry. My hands met the brick of her flesh. She fell away.

My son was climbing up my lap into my arms, putting his arms around my neck.

He said, "Mama."

The last brick fell down. I was standing there looking up through tears. I was standing by myself in the rubble of my life, at the bottom of every story I had ever needed to know. I was gripping my ribs like a climber holding on to rock. I was whispering the word over and over, and it was holding me up like a loved hand.

I can tell you anything. All you have to believe is the truth.

———

THE PHOTOGRAPHS

AUTHOR'S NOTE

Two or Three Things I Know for Sure was written for performance in the months following the completion of my novel, *Bastard Out of Carolina*. First performed in August 1991 at The Lab in San Francisco, the piece has been performed in a variety of cities and has changed with each production. For publication the work has been substantially revised. The names of most family members have been changed and other characters are composites—creations based on friends, family, and acquaintances.

Also by

Dorothy Allison

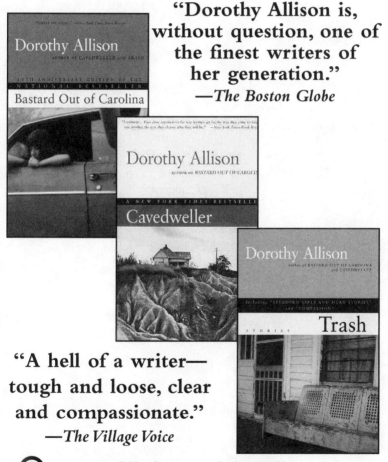

"Dorothy Allison is, without question, one of the finest writers of her generation."
—*The Boston Globe*

"A hell of a writer—tough and loose, clear and compassionate."
—*The Village Voice*